Killer Technique®: Upright Bass

by Chris Tordini

1   2

Visit us on the Web at www.melbay.com — E-mail us at email@melbay.com

Table of Contents

Introduction

My view on technique has always been that it is a means to an end. Technical virtuosity is certainly something to strive for and admire, but it does not automatically make for good music.

As it relates to improvisation, improving your technique on an instrument is a way of opening doors. You do not need to be able to play 32nd notes at 280 bpm to be a great improviser, but having better technique will help your hands express musical ideas more effectively. Being able to execute new musical ideas on the fly is what improvising musicians work towards. One part of this work should pertain to technique.

Technique on the upright bass is a very personal thing. Some players naturally have better right hand technique than left hand, and some are the opposite. We can even break down right and left hand technique into two separate categories. With the right hand, we need to think about crossing from string to string, while also controlling the speed of the index and middle fingers. Regarding the left hand, some players are naturally inclined to think up and down the neck of the bass as opposed to across the strings. This book has exercises for improving all 4 of these areas:

Right Hand
- Playing across the strings
- Speed of index and middle fingers

Left Hand
- Vertical playing (up and down the fingerboard)
- Horizontal playing (across the strings)

(This book does not talk about any technique in the thumb position.)

If we think about technique in the practice room, then ideally we will not need to think about it while performing. Technique is something to work on diligently, and then forget about completely. In the end, the point is to play beautiful music, not to impress others with our fast fingers.

(NOTE: I recommend using a metronome for ALL of the exercises in this book.)

RIGHT HAND

This first exercise is all about crossing strings with your right hand. Start nice and slow; a good starting tempo would be somewhere between 75 – 80 bpm, or even slower if you wish. As it becomes more comfortable, you should slightly increase the tempo to push yourself. One thing to concentrate on is always alternating between your index and middle fingers. First play through the exercise starting with your index finger, and then do it again starting with your middle finger.

Now let's take a look at an exercise that is designed to help control the speed of your right hand. There are constant subtle changes in rhythm, requiring you to really think about how fast your index and middle fingers are moving. The basic concept of this exercise is that there is a big pulse (around 50 – 60 bpm to start), and you must keep playing smaller and smaller subdivisions of the beat. When you get to 8 notes per beat, then you go backwards. Some of the rhythms are tricky, so just remember to play as accurately as possible. One important thing to keep in mind here is to make all of the subdivisions as even as possible. For example, if it says to play 5 notes in the beat, then really make all 5 notes just as even as you can. If you are having trouble moving between the subdivisions, I highly recommend just hanging on any or all of them until each one feels more comfortable.

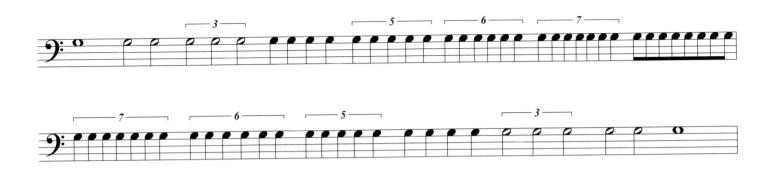

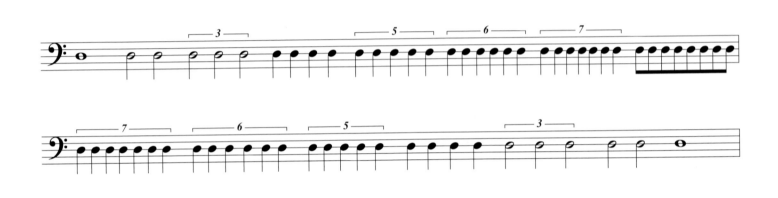

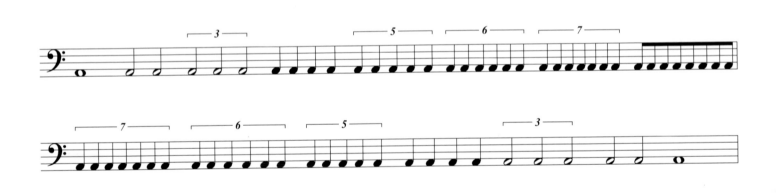

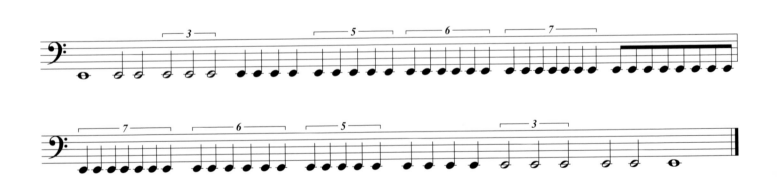

LEFT HAND

The next exercise is meant to warm up your left hand, as well as strengthen it, and confuse the fingers a little bit. As with all of the left hand exercises in this book, this one also involves the right hand, so keep that in mind as well. Continue to alternate the index and middle fingers of the right hand, and experiment with starting some exercises with the index finger and some with the middle finger. (NOTE: any of these left hand exercises can also be great arco!)

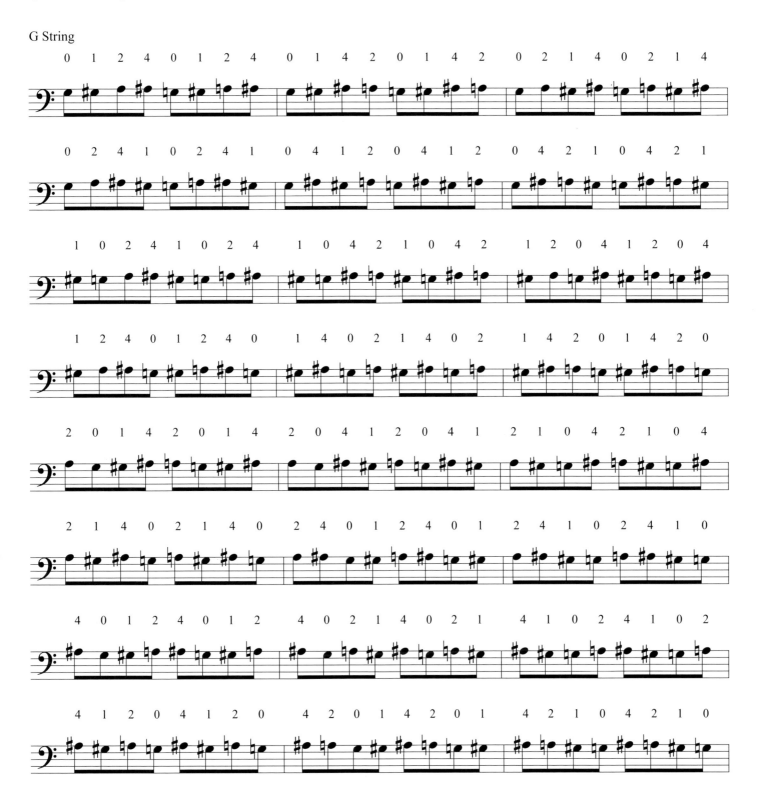

D String

A String

E String

10

In the next exercise, the idea is to play up and down the fingerboard on one string at a time. I have written out each of the 12 major scales (one octave) to be played up and down one string, starting on the G string. If the scale does not have a G♮, then it starts on A♭/G♯. The focus of this exercise is shifting, which I refer to as "vertical" playing. Try to make your shifts as smooth and seamless as possible. You will notice that I did not put left hand finger numbers in the latter part of this exercise. That is because the fingerings are the same for all four strings. Simply apply the G string fingerings to the other strings.

G String

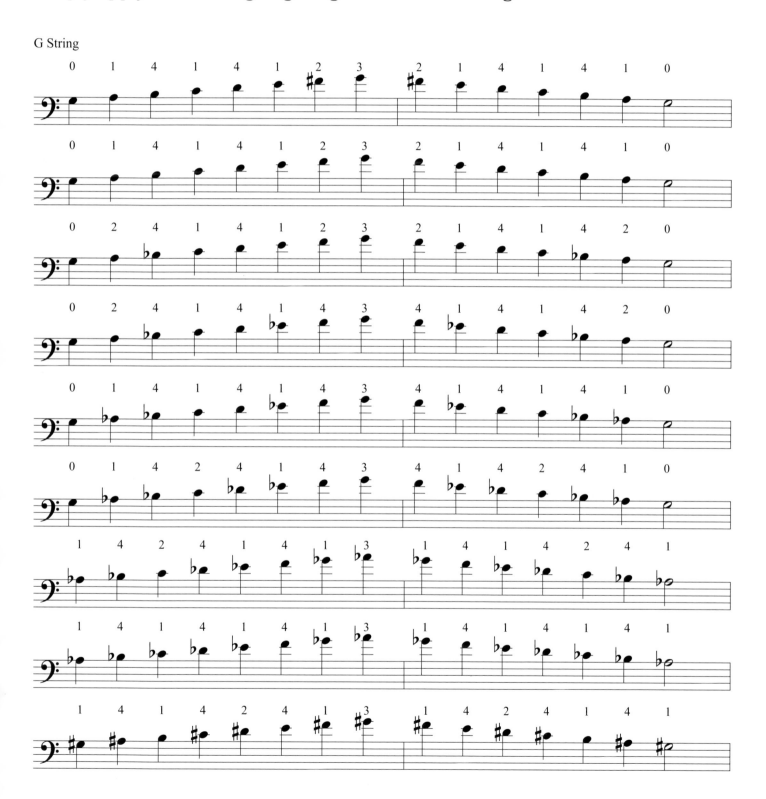

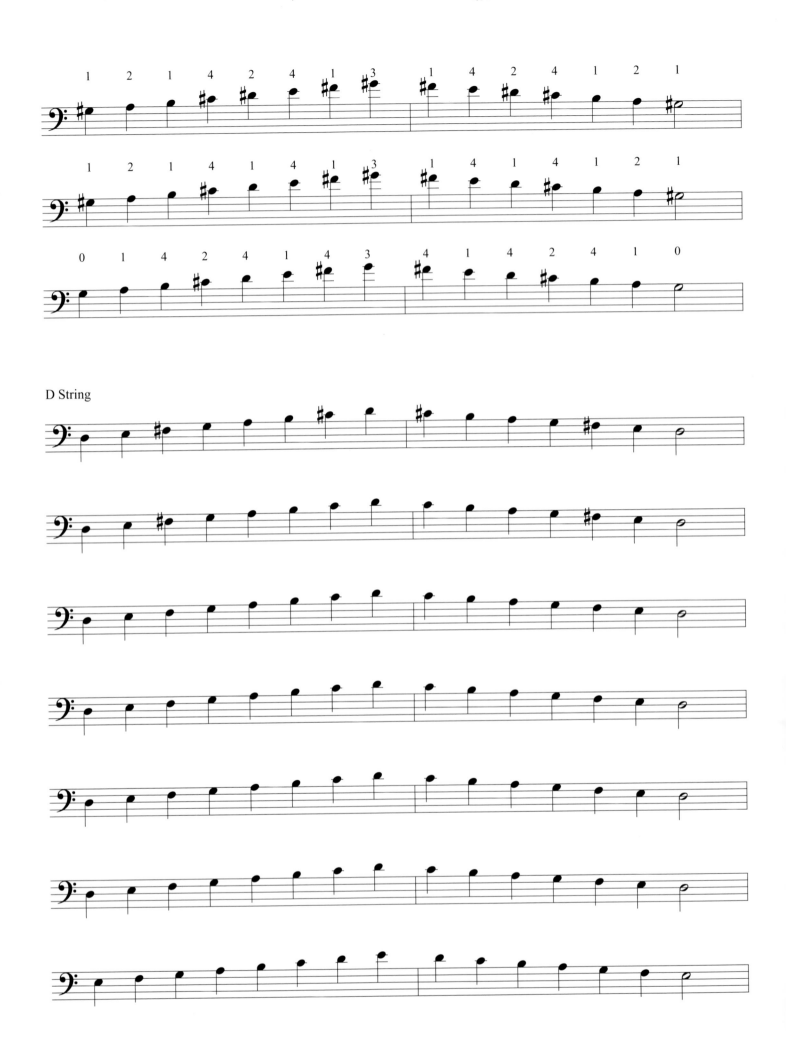

D String

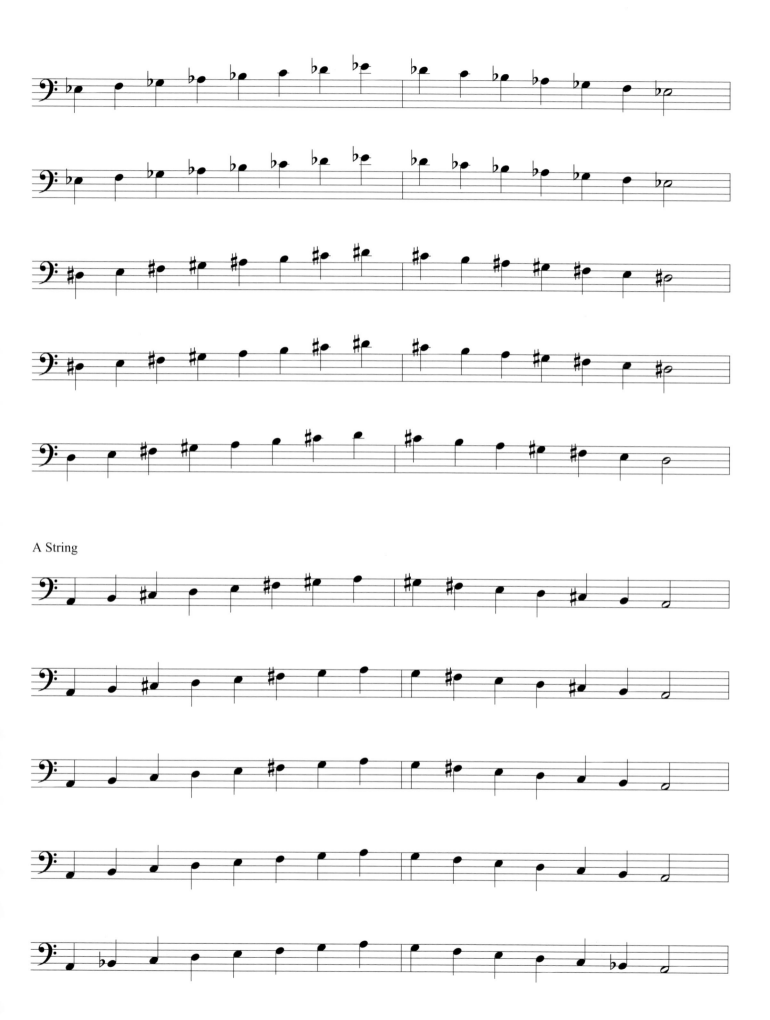

A String

13

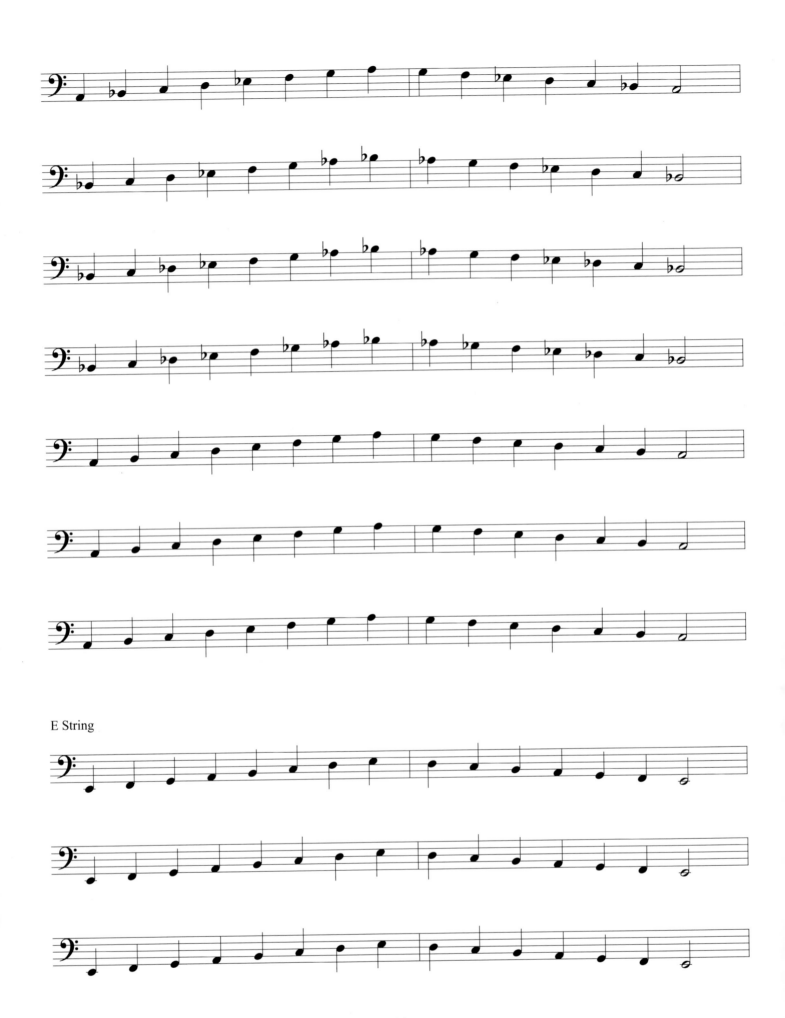

E String

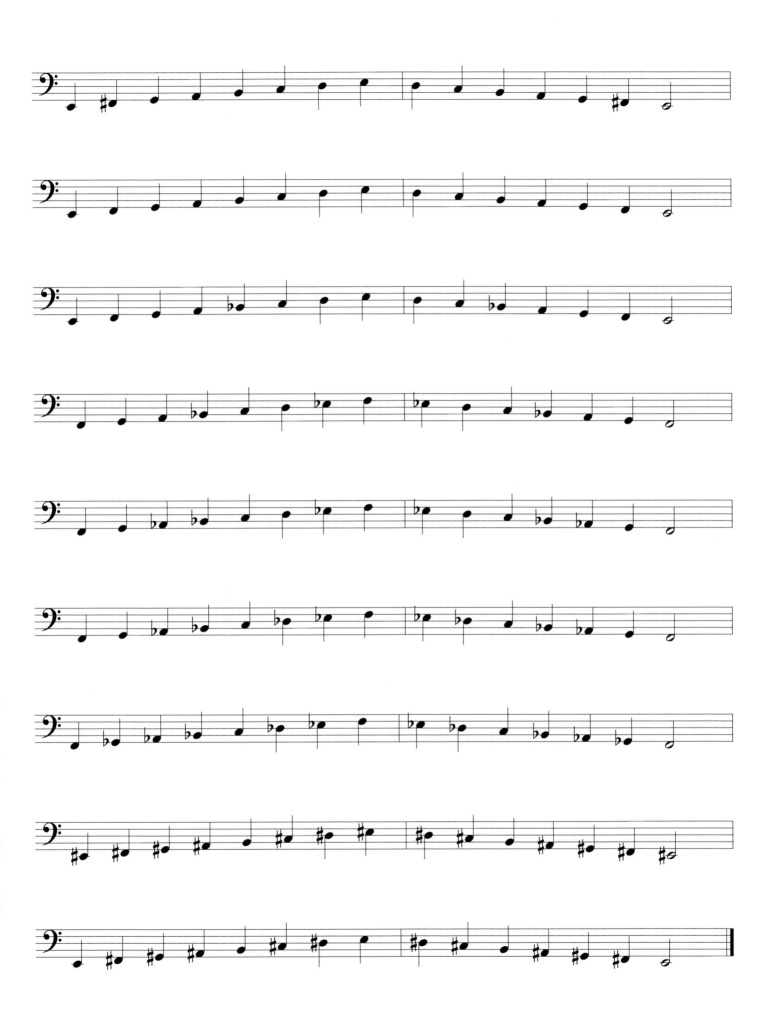

15

The next exercise should help you hone in on your ability to shift from finger to finger. The idea is to concentrate on each type of finger shift (1 to 2, 1 to 4, 2 to 1, 2 to 4, 4 to 1, and 4 to 2). A good tempo at which to start this one is around 60 – 65 bpm.

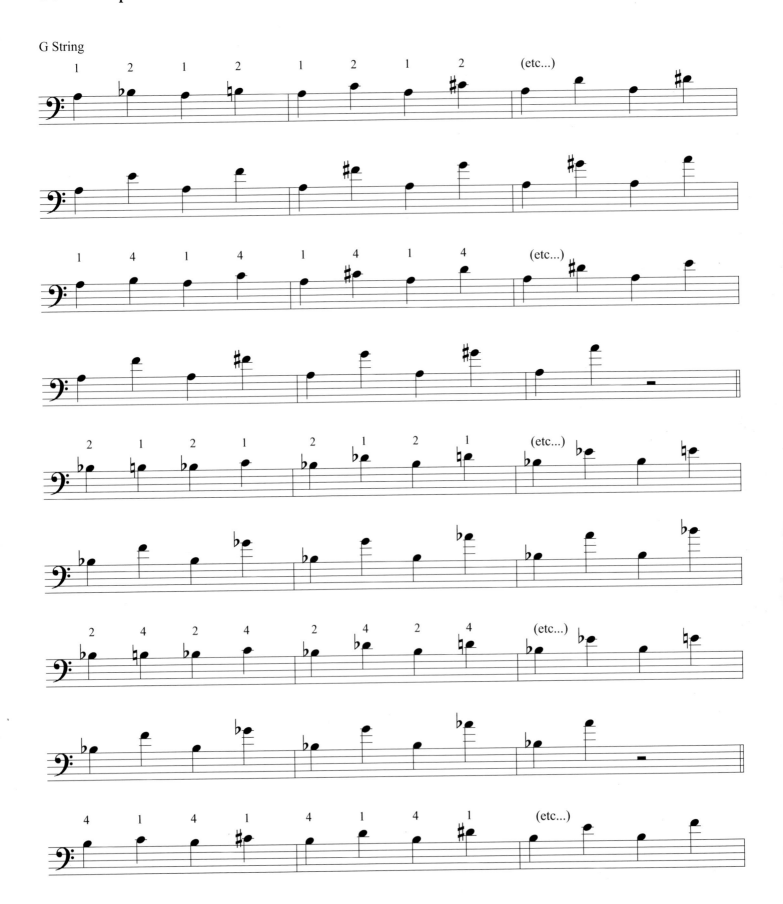

D String

A String

E String

Next we have a combination of two of our previous exercises. We are putting together the "major scale up and down a single string" one and the "different subdivisions within a larger beat" one. It is a tough one, but very rewarding to work on!

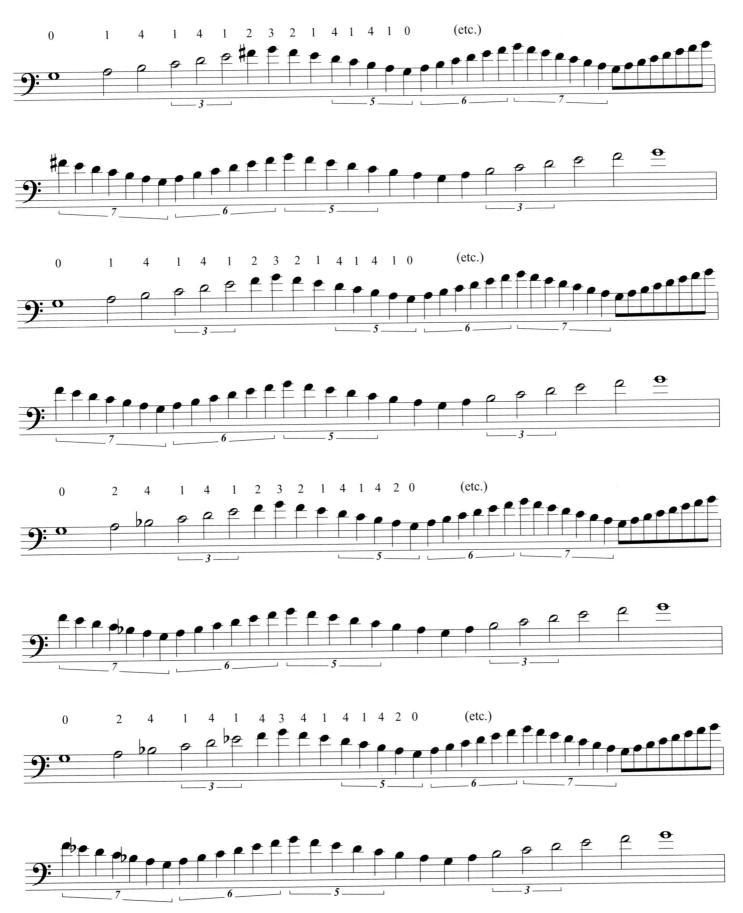

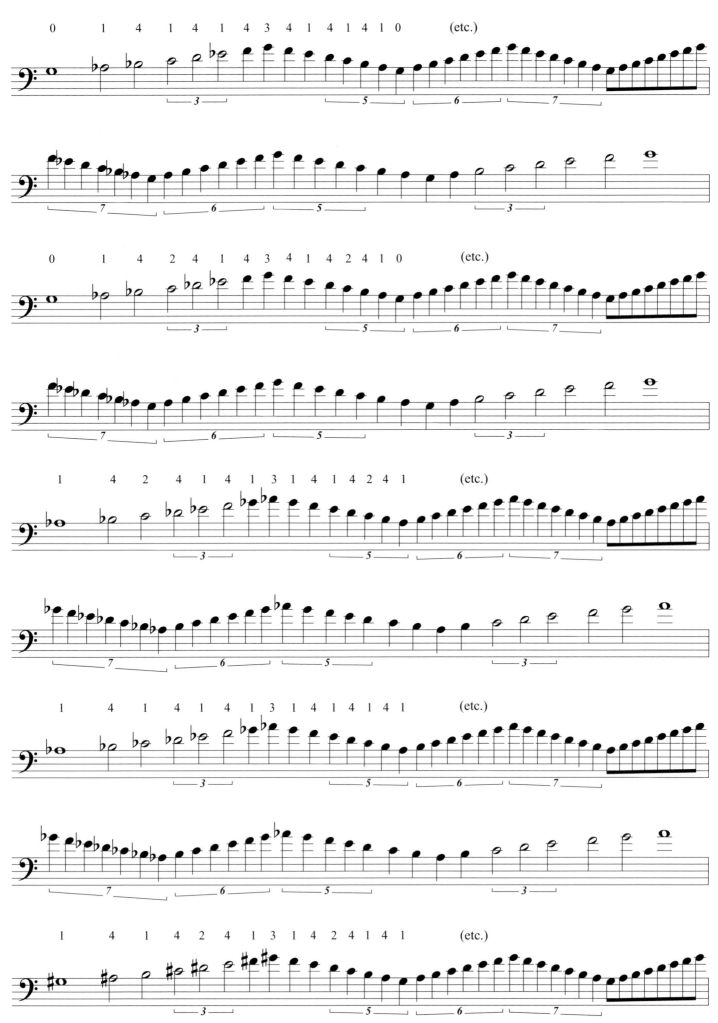

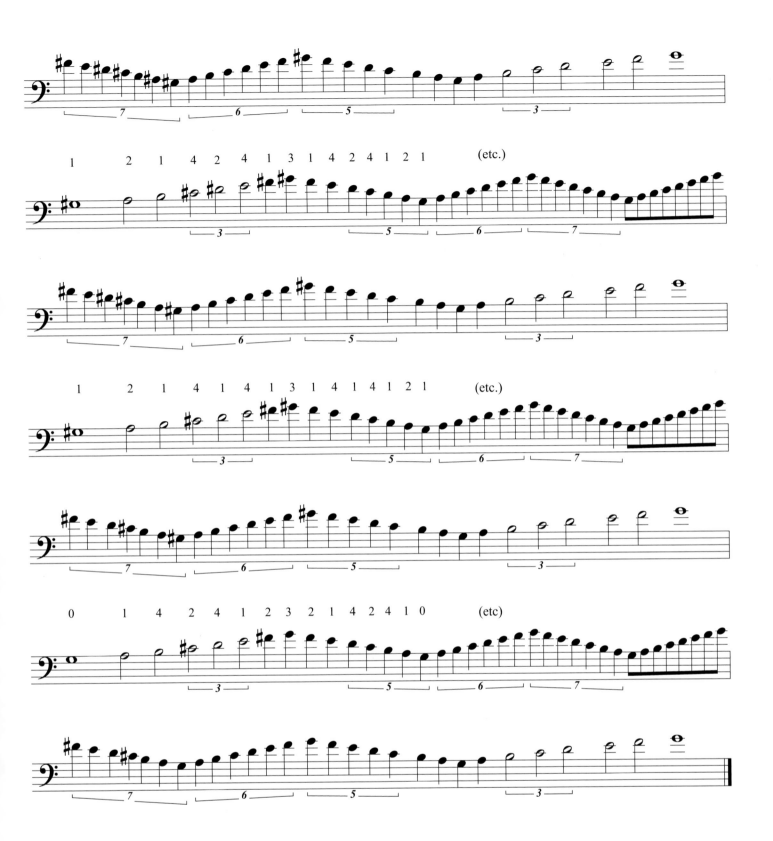

The next exercise is sort of both a shifting exercise and crossing exercise for your left hand. It is all of the major scales in 6ths, starting on the third scale degree. You may notice there are not finger numbers above the notes. This is because there are two practical ways to play 6ths on the bass, and I think you should try both while playing through this exercise. One way is to play across one string (i.e. E string to A string), while you can also play across two strings (i.e. E string to D string). Here is a small example:

Crossing two strings to play 6ths is not always possible, but I strongly encourage you to work on playing them that way when you can in this exercise. One thing to keep in mind here is to play each quarter note to its full value. When there is a lot of shifting going on, it is a common tendency to cut notes short. Try to hold on to each as long as you can before moving on to the next note. A good starting tempo for this is around 55 bpm.

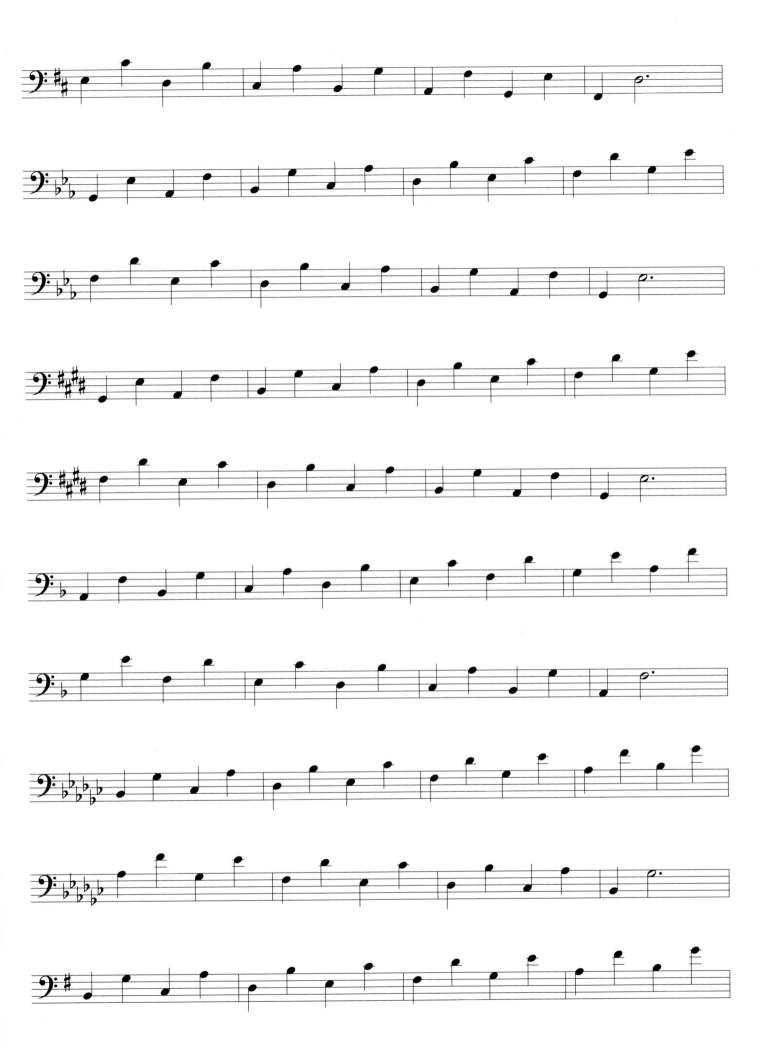

25

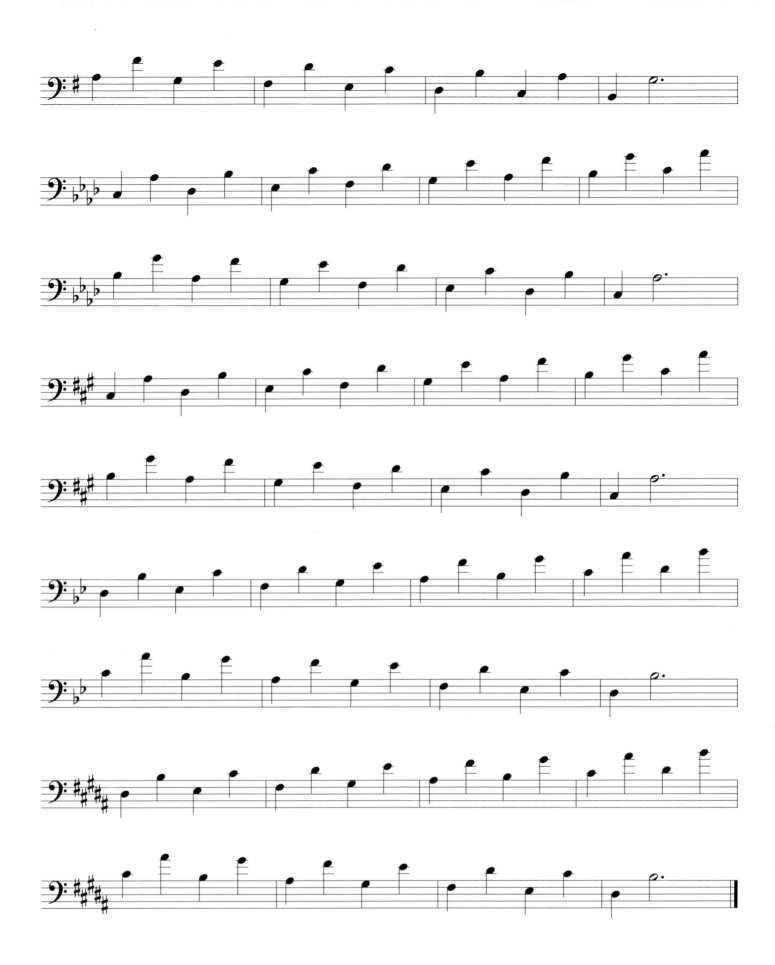

26

These final two exercises are designed to help work on string crossing with both your left hand and right hand. Take your time with each one. They are meant to tire out your fingers, so don't push yourself too hard. Think about intonation and accuracy above all else.

I sincerely hope that you have found at least a few of these exercises to be helpful in improving your technique. These exercises can be useful to you for as long as you would like them to be. There is no end for improving technique. Never stop looking!

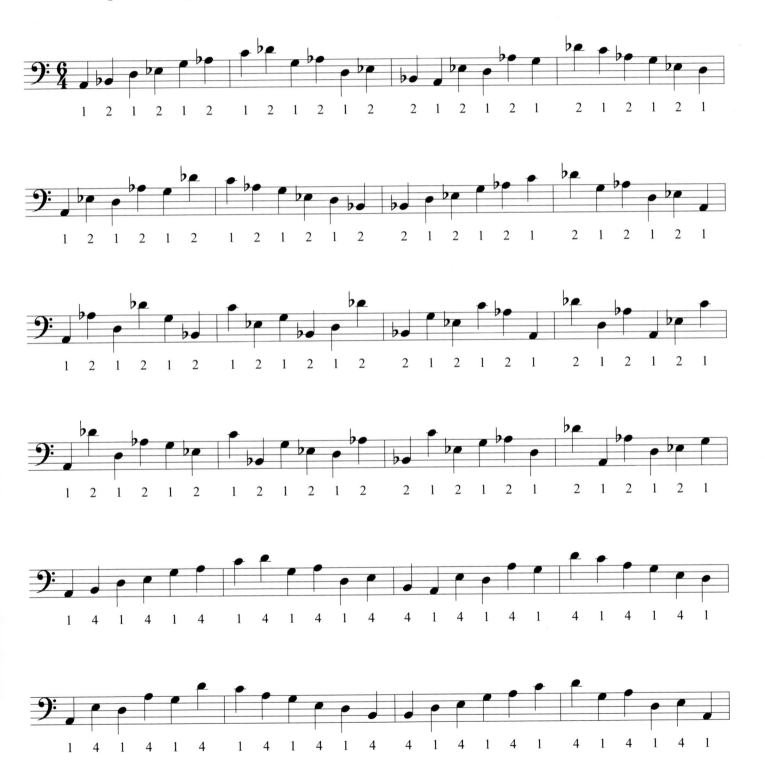

1 4 1 4 1 4 1 4 1 4 1 4 4 1 4 1 4 1 4 1 4 1 4 1 4 1

1 4 1 4 1 4 1 4 1 4 1 4 4 1 4 1 4 1 4 1 4 1 4 1 4 1

2 4 2 4 2 4 2 4 2 4 2 4 4 2 4 2 4 2 4 2 4 2 4 2 4 2

2 4 2 4 2 4 2 4 2 4 2 4 4 2 4 2 4 2 4 2 4 2 4 2 4 2

2 4 2 4 2 4 2 4 2 4 2 4 4 2 4 2 4 2 4 2 4 2 4 2 4 2

2 4 2 4 2 4 2 4 2 4 2 4 4 2 4 2 4 2 4 2 4 2 4 2 4 2

29

Notes

Notes